These Blind Eyes Now See

Marolyn Ford
with
Phyllis Boykin

VICTOR BOOKS

a division of SP Publications, Inc., Wheaton, Illinois

Offices also in Fullerton, California • Whitby, Ontario, Canada • London, England

Third printing, 1979

Scripture quotations are from the King James
Version.

Library of Congress Catalog Card No: 76-62742
ISBN: 0-88207-657-4

VICTOR BOOKS
A division of SP Publications, Inc.
P. O. Box 1825 • Wheaton, Ill. 60187

1

Going Blind

The doctor's blunt announcement shattered my world. As best I remember, he said, "You are blind and there's nothing we can do about it; go home and learn to live with it."

"Learn to live with it?" my heart and soul cried out silently. I had been learning to live with it for 10 years, yet I was not prepared for the total blindness that progressively was coming upon me.

On the long drive home with my husband, Acie, from Houston, Texas to Farmerville,

Louisiana in September 1970 there was time for thinking, time for trying to understand this darkness that would soon overtake me completely.

My mind went back to 1960 when it all started. After graduating from Holland High School in Holland, Michigan, I accepted a job as a secretary. Since Mother and I both worked in town, she would pick me up after work each day, and I would drive us home. Life was good. I was young and excited about the future, but my eyes began to fail me.

Knowing how much I enjoyed driving, Mother wondered if something was wrong when day after day I excused myself from driving. I didn't want anyone to know about my problem, so I said nothing about it. I hoped my eyesight would improve. But as it continued to fail, I became depressed, worried, and anxious.

After only three months on my secretarial job, I could no longer see well enough to do my work. When I called to another secretary to ask her to do my part, she asked, "Why?" I was so deeply concerned over my failing eyesight, that I couldn't find words to explain I was having difficulty seeing. When I was

Contents

To my parents, to whom I shall ever be grateful for the early Christian training in my life.

To my young daughter Sharon who showed much love and understanding in many little ways during the years of my blindness.

To my wonderful, loving husband, for whose strength, love, and understanding, I am so thankful.

Foreword

What words does one use to describe a miracle? When Marolyn's mother-in-law (and my sister-in-law) called to tell me about what had taken place, I was speechless. I wanted to express my feelings, but no words seemed appropriate. Instead I choked up with tears and said nothing. As though she were standing right beside me, able to read the emotion on my face, Mrs. Ford said, "That's all right, hon. I know just how you feel."

Marolyn's miracle is a big miracle, right there for everyone to see. But the Lord performs the unnoticeable as well as the noticeable miracles. I consider it a miracle that I am the co-author of this book.

Writing preschool material for the Baptist Sunday School Board of the Southern Baptist Convention for four years had been an interesting and satisfying experience. In late August 1972, however, the Lord began speaking to me during my daily devotions. He revealed to me that He had something special for me to write, something not related to the writing I was already involved in. I felt it was a book, and I was puzzled. I didn't have the knowledge or education to write about the Bible. What then did the Lord want me to write?

The feeling was so strong that more than once I sat down at the typewriter or picked up a pen and paper, only to stare at the blank pages. This frustrated me, because I knew I was to write something, but I didn't know how or where to begin. Finally I said, "Lord, I know there's something You want me to write, but I don't know what it is. I'm willing to write it, Lord. I'm waiting for You to reveal to me what it is and when to begin." The frustration left me. I even forgot about the project at times, and then again in prayer I would be reminded of it, but not with frustration. It was as if the Lord were gently saying, "Don't forget."

It was during this time that Marolyn's mother-in-law called to tell me of the miracle that had happened to Marolyn. I had often prayed that the Lord would perform this miracle, but only later did I relate the miracle to what the Lord was trying to tell me. At the same time the Lord healed Marolyn, He was speaking to me about the book.

In November 1972, about three months after the Lord had begun speaking to me about writing something, I felt I should turn down an invitation to the annual Preschool Writers' Conference in Nashville, Tennessee at the Baptist Sunday School Board. I had loved the fellowship during the four previous conferences, and would have enjoyed the writing assignments given me at this one. But the Lord said no. It was a hard thing for me to write my editor and say I would not come, for I still did not know why I felt led not to go.

On Christmas Eve of that same year, I got my answer. On that day I received a Christmas card from Marolyn Ford. Inside she had written about the testimony she was giving as she traveled to churches in various cities. She said that everywhere she went, people asked her to write a book about her life. She had prayed about it, and felt led to ask me to help her in writing this book.

It wasn't easy to write a book long distance (from Huttig, Arkansas to Huntsville, Alabama), but with the help of typewriters and tape recorders, the three of us did it—Marolyn, the Lord and I. At times it was hard work, but it was always interesting, and usually fun. It all added up to an experience I'll never forget.

Phyllis Boykin

finally able to tell her how poor my vision was, she pointed to a woman who had just entered the room. "Can you see her?" she asked.

I could hardly get the words out as I replied, "No, I can't see that far."

Admitting the seriousness of my problem, I made an appointment with our family doctor. For three weeks I visited him without my mother's knowledge; I just couldn't find the words to tell her. It would upset her, and I was afraid I would break down and cry when I told her. What might be wrong terrified me.

Finally, Mother asked me why I did not want to cook, drive, or do other little things around the house anymore. I had to tell her the truth. Calmly, I tried to tell her I could no longer see well enough to read, write, or drive a car. When I was finished, she exclaimed, "Why didn't you say so, girl? You need to see a doctor!" I fought back burning tears as I told her I had been seeing the best doctor in town!

No longer able to see to do my work, I had to quit my secretarial job. My doctor admitted me to Holland Hospital, where they ran tests and tried different medications.

Nothing worked. Then Mother took me to the Ann Arbor Medical Center on Eyes in Ann Arbor, Michigan. Later we went to the Mayo Brothers Medical Center in Rochester, Minnesota. After a thorough examination, the doctor there diagnosed my problem: macular degeneration, a hereditary loss of central vision. But I had no knowledge of it occurring in my family.

Macular degeneration works differently in different people. For me it meant I could see only the fuzzy shapes of people and tell their height and build, but I could not distinguish faces, eyes, or expressions. By straining to see the outlines of furniture and doors, I could, with some difficulty, move about without bumping into things.

The Mayo doctor assured me that the trouble in my central vision would never affect my side vision. He explained that I would have problems at first because the macular degeneration was new, and I was still trying to see straight forward. But he assured me I would see a little better when I learned to use my side vision.

The condition could not be improved with glasses, however, and I was considered legally blind. I was frightened, shocked, and unwilling to believe this was really happening to me.

I felt like a cripple; my body had become imperfect. I felt strange and helpless; I had lost the ability to fit in without being different. The importance of physical perfection emphasized by the world now made me feel insecure. Blindness was more than a loss of vision; it was an attack on my self-image. It meant more than losing my eyesight; it meant dying to the only way of life I had ever known.

Some things were just too painful to talk about. The inability to see my mother's smile, a child's face, another human being—or even myself—made acceptance very difficult.

I could no longer watch television, catch the writings on billboards and signs, find a phone number in the telephone book, or read books of any kind—it was a grievous adjustment. I could no longer stay alert to the changing times, new hair styles, fashions, and makeup trends. Changes in landscaping and buildings went unnoticed. Friends and relatives tried to keep me aware of changes, but I could not visualize them. It was difficult to imagine from other people's descriptions, no matter how expertly given, just what they were trying to say. I could not see their gestures, the nodding of their heads, the shrugging of their shoulders, their posture, or their facial expressions. I felt as though I was missing half of every conversation. I was standing still while around me the whole world was moving ahead.

Whether a person goes blind slowly due to disease, or quickly because of an accident, he must face bottom before he can start the long climb up. He must be told the truth. I had to learn to accept my blindness, whether it was temporary or permanent. I didn't have to like it, but with the Lord's help, I had to accept it. Only then could I begin to remake and rehabilitate my life. Often I prayed in all earnestness: "Lord, if I have to be blind, please let it be for a purpose. Somehow may God be glorified through it."

Most young girls just out of high school have a promising future as they start a career, go to college, find a husband. I didn't need anything like blindness coming over me . . . not at this young age. Who would want to marry a blind girl? What would I do with my life? How was I going to handle this problem? It was an insurmountable obstacle, and I felt defeated.

In my valley of self-pity, I realized I had to learn to cope with my blindness, and make my life fulfilling. I asked the Lord to help me with it hour by hour and day by day.

The first struggle to rehabilitate myself was to learn a new way of recognizing people, for I could no longer see clearly enough to recognize faces. I had to start noticing forms and outlines, and learn to distinguish one from the other. I had to find new ways of doing everything.

While looking for ways to occupy myself, I heard about a widower with two sons who was looking for a cook-housekeeper. My parents thought I might be able to handle the job, but I felt insecure about it. I had begun learning how to cook again, but the responsibility of cooking for a man and two boys and cleaning a house in new surroundings seemed to be asking too much. Yet I felt compelled to take the job. I wanted to prove to myself that I could handle the situation. So every day I cleaned the house, made the beds, and cooked dinner and supper for them. I enjoyed the work, but I felt totally incapable of handling the situation. In a few weeks, I gave it up.

People in my home church prayed for me

for months; some continued praying for me through the years that followed. One mother told me that her little daughter was so worried and concerned about me that she remembered me in her prayers nightly.

I thanked God for those prayers, but the psychological shock of becoming blind affected my emotional stability.

I had always been quiet and serious-minded; now I became even more withdrawn, always deep in thought, hiding my blindness and my feelings.

During this emotional trauma, a man from the Lions Club came out to fit me with a white cane. I refused it; if a white cane would make me look blind, helpless, and dependent, I didn't want it. I did, however, buy the braille watch he showed me, and found it a tremendous blessing to be able to tell time once again.

Another helpful and encouraging man came regularly from the Rehabilitation Center. He suggested that I become a dictaphone typist for the government, because the pay was good and I would not have to depend on my eyes to do the work. I thought about it, but felt that typing hour after hour was just not for me.

I was approached about learning braille, but I wasn't ready to admit I was blind. I would not learn braille.

To fill the lonely hours, I began riding to the city with Mother. I would walk about town, shopping while she worked; then we would ride home together. "Pretending to shop" would be more accurate, for while I could find my own way into the stores, I could not purchase anything without the help of a salesperson. Often I would not ask for help in finding out the size or price of an article because I didn't want to admit I was blind. Very soon those shopping expeditions became boring and frustrating.

Near Mother's place of work were several trampolines. To help time pass more quickly, I would go with her sometimes and jump on the trampolines for fun and exercise. It was the one thing I found enjoyable while waiting for Mother to finish work.

Music was another welcome way to pass time. I had taken lessons when I was young, but I had not learned much more than the scales. After losing my central vision, I did not know at first what to do with all the time on my hands. Depressed and frustrated, I would sit day after day with the record player on, listening to gospel and sacred singing. I especially loved listening to J. T. Adams and the Men of Texas. The music took my mind off myself and put my thoughts on heavenly things. My heart would go up in prayer to the Lord as I gave my troubles to Him.

2

Love
Isn't Blind

More than anything I wanted to attend Tennessee Temple College in Chattanooga, Tennessee where my twin sister, Carolyn, was studying. I wrote to Dr. Lee Roberson, president of the school, asking if I could enroll. I explained that though I could not see to read textbooks or write exams, I would be able to do my work by recording class lectures on tapes and studying them. With hope in my heart, I mailed the letter, and then prayed every day that I would be accepted if it was what the Lord wanted for me.

In a few weeks the answer came: I was accepted. I could attend Tennessee Temple, but on one condition. Before enrolling I would have to ask each teacher if he or she would be willing to give me oral tests. This meant additional responsibility for the instructors; they would have to cover all the material in the classroom discussions since I could not read the books. I was to enroll in January 1961, and I knew everything would work out. I was positive this was the Lord's will. In November 1960, I went to "look" at the Tennessee Temple's campus and to visit my sister Carolyn.

Carolyn was dating a young man by the name of Hersholt Ford, so it was natural that I should meet him and his brother Acie. What I hadn't expected was a deep-down feeling that Acie was the answer to my prayers.

Since the age of 13 I had been praying for my husband-to-be, whoever and wherever he was. One night as my family and I were driving the seven miles home from church, I had heard Billy Graham say in a radio sermon: "Young person, you may be only 13 years of age, but now is the time to begin

praying for your life partner." Every day
after that, I prayed for my future husband.
As I worked in the hay fields of our farm, I
prayed for his character, his personality, and
his safety. I prayed that the Lord would
make him a man of God, a man of prayer, a
man of kindness, compassion, and understanding. My character and personality were
also being developed, so I prayed that our
lives would be so interwoven that when the
Lord led us together, we would be able to do
a wonderful work for Him. I also knew the
Lord had called me to be a pastor's wife.

On that first meeting, of course, I did not
tell Acie that the Lord seemed to say, "Marolyn, this is the one you have been praying for
all these years." I didn't know him, and be-
sides, he was dating Carolyn's roommate
(who later became my roommate). Yet there
seemed to be a bond of understanding and
closeness between us. We were drawn to one
another by a mutual feeling of deep respect.

I was unable to see Acie's features, but he
was unaware of this. He only knew I was
legally blind, that I could not see to read and
write. Like others, he didn't know the extent
of my blindness because I worked so hard to
cover it up. I wore glasses then, and most

people assumed that the glasses helped my vision. They didn't; they only gave me something to hide behind. (Since I could not see my face, I was never sure I had my eyebrows marked right. The frames of the glasses covered up those errors I made in applying makeup.)

On the first evening of my visit to Tennessee Temple, Carolyn, Hersholt, Acie, Acie's sister Hazel, and I went to the dating parlor. We all had a wonderful time with one another, especially Acie and I, as we talked and became better acquainted.

Next morning after breakfast, Acie asked me for our first date. He said he would pick me up at 7 that evening. I was thrilled about having a date with this wonderful and handsome (so I had been told) man I had just met. At lunch I found a seat at a table, and suddenly Acie was sitting beside me. We dated every night that week. The more we learned about each other, the sweeter our friendship became. Acie seemed to possess those qualities I had prayed for in the man God had for me. He was kind, understanding, sincere, and most important, he loved the Lord dearly.

All too soon the week ended. I went back

to Michigan to wait until the January semester when I was to enroll in school. Acie and I corresponded during the month of December (I typed my letters to him as I couldn't see to write). When I returned in January, I had a small gift for him—a tie clasp. We were sitting in the dating parlor again, only this time he was telling me that he had his eye on a girl he wanted to ask out. Just as he spoke the girl's name, she appeared in the parlor. "There she is now," he said. My heart was crushed, but still I knew inside that someday we would be married.

My major in Bible consumed hour after hour. Studying by tape recorder was difficult, and for every hour I spent in class, I would have to spend at least two hours listening and relistening to the tapes, trying to learn the material just from hearing it spoken. The instructors were most kind and understanding. They allowed me to leave the room during oral tests, and after class they would spend 15 to 20 minutes asking me the same questions.

Because I had to answer orally, I was at first intimidated by students who waited around to listen to me give answers or to talk with the instructor. I studied hard for these tests and for class because I didn't want to be embarrassed by not knowing the answers. My diligence resulted in very good grades. Yet I couldn't have done it without the Lord's help and encouragement.

Most of the students didn't know I was blind because I could successfully hide my poor vision. I looked and acted like any sighted person, but how I longed to clearly see people and things, to be able to read text-books and written exams. I wanted desperately to graduate from Tennessee Temple, but that was not possible. My limited vision prevented me from completing some of the courses.

When I was not studying Bible or music, I was studying Acie Ford. I wanted to know his strengths and weaknesses and understand his moods and mannerisms. I wanted to know when he needed encouragement and a listening ear. Like any young woman after a man, I sought opportunities to talk with him.

Because Acie worked as a clothing sales-man in a local store, he got off work too late to eat in the dining hall on campus. He always ate at a campus restaurant, the Happy Corner. I knew if I worked there I could see Acie often, so I applied for a job and was accepted. My eyesight was a problem till I learned where everything was, but I was determined to try to hold on to the job. While all the students were eating their meals on campus, Acie and I had precious times sharing our hearts with each other.

I learned that Acie had first dedicated his life to the Lord when he was 10 years old. Even then he knew the Lord was calling him into fulltime Christian service, yet he often walked the aisle seeking to know God's will.

One day during the summer following his high school graduation, he was driving around with his friend, Phil Rogers. Acie had preregistered at Northeast Louisiana State College, where Phil had attended the previous year. Thinking of the future, Acie said, "I believe God wants something different for me." Phil answered, "You need to do what He wants you to do."

That night Acie talked with Phil's father, the Rev. W. R. Rogers, who told him of Tennessee Temple College. Acie respected his opinion, for it was under his ministry that he had grown up and accepted the call to preach. So Acie enrolled at Tennessee Temple in September, not knowing how he would pay tuition and other expenses. One week after school began he found work in one of the downtown clothing stores. Acie took this to be an indication of God's approval.

One day, in 1960 as Acie was in the prayer tower talking with the Lord and reading his Bible, his eyes fell on Matthew 5:6: "Blessed are they which do hunger and thirst after righteousness, for they shall be filled." Acie had no more doubts that he had been called to preach the Gospel.

At the time I had prayed for my future husband, whoever he would be, I had also prayed for my in-laws. I had prayed that they would love and accept me, and that we would have a sweet and lovely relationship. God answered that prayer.

Even before Acie's and my relationship became serious, I fell in love with his parents, Virginia and Willard Ford. They came to visit him, and wanting to get better acquainted with me, they invited me to go out with them for the afternoon and evening. Should I go or shouldn't I? Acie had a date with another girl that night, and I didn't want him to think that I was chasing him by visiting with his family all evening. Mr. Ford insisted, though, saying that he would let Acie know I was there at his request and not for any other reason. The Fords and I had a wonderful time. It was as if we had known each other for years. Later Acie told us that the entire time he was out with his date that night, he was wishing he could be with us. That incident, along with the fact that another young man had asked me to marry him, opened Acie's eyes to his true feelings about me.

As Acie and I became more serious, we had long talks about our feelings toward each other. Acie thought that perhaps it wasn't love he felt for me, but pity because of my blindness. We discussed the fact that though my condition was not expected to get worse, anything could happen where a weakness already existed. In time, it was love we felt for each other.

The day came when I happily called my parents to tell them Acie and I were planning to be married in the summer. I admired their attitude; they didn't ask me, "Are you sure this is the right fellow? Can he support you?" They seemed to feel that if this was my choice, then it was all right with them. Perhaps they felt as though they already knew Acie. I had written them weekly, telling them all about him in my typewritten letters.

They met him for the first time two days before the wedding.

We were married August 14, 1962, and I was finally able to tell Acie how the Lord had seemed to say to me on the day we met, "This is the one you have been praying for." Our wedding was a beautiful church ceremony with a large reception. Mother worked out most of the details: the flower and candle arrangements and the dress colors and patterns. My future mother-in-law sewed every stitch of my wedding dress, a white floor-length gown with a long train floating behind. I often worried about the dress not fitting because she had never sewn for me before, but she assured me that it would fit because she was praying with every stitch. She was right; it fit, and I was pleased. At the reception dinner, my brother, Don, and his wife, Clara did a splendid job as master and mistress of ceremonies. Everything went beautifully.

Our plans for the honeymoon were to visit Canada. We drove from Holland, Michigan to Grand Rapids, Michigan, where at 1 a.m. our borrowed car refused to go any farther. We walked to a nearby motel and banged on the door, trying to wake the manager. A hippie-looking fellow heard us, and said he was about to leave, and offered us his room. We declined his offer, but asked if he would drive us into Grand Rapids to find a place to get the car fixed. He took us to an all-night wrecker service several miles from the motel. I'll never forget getting into that dirty wrecker on my honeymoon night with my "going away" outfit on—a navy blue and white dress, a corsage, white gloves, and a hat. My skirt was straight, and I could not step up into the high cab of the wrecker; Acie had to lift me.

We were back at the motel by 2 o'clock. The manager was awake this time, and gave us a room. After locking me safely in our room, Acie went back with the mechanic to get the car fixed. On the way back to the motel he became completely lost in the unfamiliar surroundings, but finally found his way to the motel at 4 A.M., with the car repaired. I had already gone to bed. Acie came in, started to put on his pajamas, and found that someone had machine-sewn the arms and legs together. We laughed and laughed as we sat and picked out the threads.

The next day we headed for Ontario, Canada, as we had planned, but after we crossed the United States-Canadian border, we changed our minds. Heavy rains backed up traffic for miles. Everyone spoke French, but we could tell by signs along the way that gasoline and motel rates were very high. Having already spent a good bit of our money on the car, we didn't have much left. As evening came we began looking for a motel, but after talking it over, we decided to save money by going back to the States.

It took us hours to get back on the ferry. At least 200 cars were waiting to cross. When we were finally on the other side, we drove for miles and miles, but not a gas station, restaurant, or motel was in sight. Just when we felt we could drive no farther, we saw a sign that read "20 miles" to a motel. We made it somehow, but what a disappointment when we arrived! The "motel" was just a small roadside inn without a restaurant. We didn't eat until later the next morning.

Acie summed up our feelings the next day when he suggested, "Let's go back to your mama's so we can get a good night's sleep and some good food."

3

Toward
Total Darkness

Despite the unfortunate circumstances, our
marriage was off to a wonderful start. After
the honeymoon, we drove back to Tennessee
Temple where we moved into a second-floor
apartment just off campus. In June of the
next year Acie graduated from Tennessee
Temple with a Bachelor of Theology degree.
We then moved to Grand Rapids, Michigan,
where Acie enrolled in the Grand Rapids
Baptist Bible College. He worked his way
through school as a clothing salesman while

we attended Rose Park Baptist Church where Acie had been asked to work as youth director.

Meanwhile, I was learning how to use my side vision. We needed extra income to pay the tuition, so I looked for work. There wasn't much I could do with my limited vision, but I located work at a pharmacy soda fountain. Having been trained for secretarial work, I felt out of place, but I had to keep on because the salary helped supply our need at the time. When the work became too great a strain on my eyes I had to quit.

Acie graduated from Grand Rapids Baptist Bible College in June, 1965.

We had been told it was best for a young minister to pastor a small church for a short time between his college and seminary education. In this way he would learn what to study in seminary, and his education would mean much more to him. That is what we did. Two months after graduation in Grand Rapids we were called to the Bosco Baptist Church in Monroe, Louisiana, where we pastored for a year. It was at this church that Acie was ordained and licensed into the ministry, and it was here that I suffered my first miscarriage.

In 1966, the Lord led us back to Tennessee Temple in Chattanooga, where Acie enrolled in seminary to work on a master's degree. We arrived in Chattanooga without money and without knowing where we would live, or where Acie would work. The only thing we were sure of was that the Lord was leading us, and that where He leads, He provides. When we arrived in Chattanooga, we went to the home of some friends who gave us the name of a woman renting apartments near the school. We called her and found she had just built a duplex. One side had been rented to a couple who were Temple students, and the other was available for rent at a reasonable price. We moved in and it was just beautiful! Everyday Acie walked downtown to look for work. The Lord was good; Acie found work as a salesman in one of the downtown clothing stores.

I also enrolled in Temple. The first time I had enrolled as a Bible major. This time I enrolled as a music major, and loved it!

Though my ability to see had improved somewhat because I had learned to use my side vision, I found my music harmony class very difficult. I studied hard to stay on the honor roll, but I had to hold my paper to my face to see what I was doing. I would do my homework and find out the next morning when another student looked over it, that the music notes weren't on the lines of the staff at all. In my other music classes I did not do paper work; the teachers understood my vision problem and helped me to do my work orally.

I went as far as I could go in my music training. A year before graduation I had to discontinue it at school, but I continued to study music at home. It meant a great deal to me as a hobby, and it was always a blessing in our church work.

On February 22, 1968, during our last year at Tennessee Temple, a new Ford came into our lives. Acie chose the name "Sharon Marie" for our seven-pound, ten-ounce baby girl. I knew she was a blue-eyed blond only because Acie described her features to me, for all I could see was a little form, an outline, a bundle of flesh. Sharon added so much to our lives!

During his seminary days, Acie had many opportunities to preach each week in services he held at the nursing home, children's home, jail, city mission, and detention home for teenagers. After he finished his graduate work at Tennessee Temple Seminary we began to candidate for a pastorate.

Two churches called us during the same week. One was a small church in Louisiana, which could offer only a part-time position. Acie would have to take a secular job if we accepted this church's call. The other church was a larger one in Kentucky which offered a full-time position. We prayed about the decision, and felt led to take the smaller church in Louisiana. We moved in September, 1968 to take up our pastorate at the Cross Roads Baptist Church in Farmerville, Louisiana, where we lived for four years.

During the second year of our ministry in Cross Roads, my peripheral vision began giving me trouble. My central vision had been gone for 10 years, but I had learned to use my side vision so well that most people could not tell that I was partially blind. Now I was faced with a greater problem. The remaining vision which I had come to depend upon was rapidly leaving me.

Soon I could no longer recognize forms and outlines of people and large objects. Most frustrating was the fact that I could not recognize individuals. At first I could still see well enough that I didn't walk into people, but finding a particular individual was almost impossible. I continued as music director at the church, but I could seldom locate the persons with whom I wanted to speak concerning special music for future services. Sometimes I heard them speaking to someone after choir practice, and if I hurried I could catch them. This manner of locating individuals caused me a great deal of tension, so I began making my contacts by telephone, even though it often meant long-distance calling.

Music was an enjoyable part of my work. My choir consisted of about 25 people, who did not care to repeat songs they had sung. Each week I had to have a new song prepared for choir practice. Early each week I began preparation for the Sunday evening choir practice. I picked from a record the song I felt led to use. If I did not have a record with a particular song on it, I would borrow it from a friend, and record the song on tape. Then as I played it back, I sat at the piano, finding the key it was written in, picking out the notes, getting the correct timing, and memorizing the words. I spent about two hours each day working on my music; I had the words and music memorized by Thursday in order to spend Friday and Saturday reviewing the song. By the time I met the choir Sunday evening, I was well-prepared.

Other things couldn't be practiced or memorized well enough to make my blindness hardly noticeable. I was hesitant to invite guests in for a meal because I could not hide my blindness if I served a meal. I would have to clear the dishes off the table before serving the dessert, but I couldn't find the dishes without my guests noticing the fact that I had to feel around for them. I had such a hang-up about clearing the dishes off the table if a sighted person were nearby that I waited to do it until after even Acie left the dining area. When I did have guests over, I preferred to serve only coffee—I could manage that.

We knew I had a whole new problem in addition to macular degeneration, and something had to be done about it. I went to my doctor and he referred me to a medical center in Houston.

I'll always remember the fear I felt as we arrived at the center. I was afraid of my surroundings. I couldn't see more than an outline of the hospital. I wasn't sure of where I was walking. I couldn't see the facial expression of the doctors. I was afraid for myself. What was wrong? Was it a passing thing? Something the doctors could correct? Or were my eyes permanently damaged? These questions haunted me till I was tied in knots.

The week of extensive tests yielded bitter results. I was going totally blind, and there was no way the doctors could help me: no treatments, no surgery, nothing! There was no hope. I felt desperate, terrified. I had learned to live with partial blindness, but total blindness was so much harder to accept.

Even with limited vision I had been able to handle my duties as a pastor's wife. I had taught a Sunday school class, directed choir, and played the piano when necessary. Through the years of being blind with macular degeneration, I had learned to do everything I needed to do as a wife and mother. I was able to cook, clean, and care for my family. And through it all my understanding, gentle, and kind husband was a strength and comfort.

But now I was fast losing the ability to see the forms of people, furniture, and doorways. Life would have to be altered again because of my eyes. We would have to learn to live with it. I clung to Romans 8:28: "We know that all things work together for good to them that love God. . . ." We knew the Lord would help, but in quiet desperation we wondered what would happen when I reached total darkness.

4

Family Life

On the way back to Farmerville, I thought about how it had been when my vision was clear, and my life uncomplicated by blindness.

On the farm where I grew up, one could see for miles across the flatlands of Michigan. It was exciting to watch the sky! Many times we saw the thunder clouds rolling in, and we would run out to be sure the farm implements were in the barn and the barn doors securely fastened before the storm began.

Tornadoes were often sighted in the area. Word would come to the little red-brick, two-room schoolhouse that we were to go home immediately. There were only five pupils in my class: two boys and three girls from kindergarten through the eighth grade. With eyes wide with fright, we would run all the way home as fast as our little legs could carry us, praying all the way that the tornado would not hit home before we did.

One day a tornado did hit our farm. Dad and the boys had secured the doors and windows and made sure the machinery was in the barn. The disastrous winds, meanwhile, were building in strength and speed. My brother Victor was tightening the front barn door next to the hay bales. Suddenly the door blew open. Roger backed the tractor against it for support. Then together, Roger and Victor tried to open the door between the cow stalls and the hay loft. Roger pulled on one side, and Victor pushed on the other, but the wind was so fierce that the door would not budge. While they struggled there in the barn, pushing and pulling, the tornado hit, and split the 80-foot barn right down the middle. The tornado not only broke every window in our house, but covered our living room floor with hail stones and debris, and shattered every window in the barn, chicken houses, and granary; fifty windows in all. The storm could have done much more damage, but the Lord protected us, and not one of the nine members of our family was hurt.

In winter, blizzard winds would blow so hard that at times we hardly made the mile-and-one-half walk home from school. Our noses would turn icy-red from the cold, and the whirling snowflakes would catch and freeze in our hair and eyebrows. Many times the snow was so deep that people could no longer shovel their way through the roads, and if northern people like us became snow-bound, that meant it was a deep snowfall!

During the summer months, my twin sister, Carolyn, and I earned spending money by picking blueberries on a farm two miles from ours. When the blueberries weren't in season, there was plenty of work to be done on our farm. I enjoyed working in the fields, especially at haying time, with our brother Roger, who was a year and one half older than Carolyn and I. During haying time we would go out early in the morning with the hay baler and tractor and trailer, and work until dark. We did what was called custom work: going to the fields of other farmers, and cutting their wheat and hay.

I loved nature; the smell of fresh-cut hay and fresh-worked soil was invigorating. I felt close to the Lord when I worked in the fields, and I prayed as I worked. Sometimes, with my heart full of praise and adoration for the Lord, I sang as we rode the machinery back and forth across the wide open fields.

I was nine years old when I began thinking seriously about accepting the Lord. I had never made that decision; I knew Jesus was coming back and I did not want to be left behind. I finally got enough courage to speak to my mother about it. We were doing the dishes. Mother was washing, as she always did, and it was my week to dry the dishes—Carolyn and I took turns drying them and clearing the table. After we finished, I asked Mother if she would go into the living room and pray with me so I could ask Jesus to come into my heart. She read from the Bible John 3:16: "For God so loved the world, that He gave His only begotten Son, that whosoever believeth in Him should not perish, but have everlasting life", and Romans 3:23: "For all have sinned and come short of the glory of God." As we prayed, I asked Jesus to come into my life. He forgave my sins, and made me one of His children.

My brothers were outside—it was a beautiful spring evening—and my mother informed me that I should go and tell them the decision I had just made. I rode my bike around and around trying to work up courage to tell my four big brothers that I had just accepted Jesus as my personal Saviour. Just before dark, I quickly told them, and then ran off, not waiting to hear what they might say!

There were seven of us children growing up together. Four boys had come first—Donald, Richard, Victor, and Roger. Then my identical twin, Carolyn, and I were born, followed five years later by our sister, Virginia. When it came time for fun and games, we always had enough team members! Carolyn, Virginia, and I played dolls every day of the week, but when we played as a family, it had to be at games the boys liked best, because they were older. Baseball, football, and basketball were at the top of their list, along with one other game we all loved to play in the winter: "Tick in the Tunnels." We made long tunnels with many different openings all through the hay bales in the barn, ran across the beams, jumped from the scaffold to a bag hanging in the center of the barn twelve feet off the ground, swung to the other side, and jumped into the bales. In the spring we played "Seven Steps around the House," and took turns on our big swing hanging across the creek in the woods near our home.

We were reared in a Christian home by dedicated parents. Family devotions were held at each meal: morning, noon, and night. We children were taught to pray around the table. The Bible was read regularly. Dad would read a whole chapter, and read it slowly, no matter how big a hurry we were in! When the church doors were open, we were there. It made no difference if homework conflicted with Revival Week; all nine of us were there every night.

Mother and Dad were wonderful parents. They loved us all deeply and equally. Mom was one of the most loving mothers in the world. She worked hard to have things nice for us. We always came first, often to the extent that she would have to do without the things she needed or wanted. We never had the slightest question in our minds about her love for us. By her example of love and affection, along with firm discipline, she greatly influenced our development and love for each other.

Dad showed his love for us in little ways. Often when we would come in from hoeing the garden or working all day in the hot blistering fields, Dad would have ready a juicy, cool watermelon for us to eat. His smile would stretch from ear to ear.

Dad's life centered around the Scriptures and his desire for people to be saved. Often as he talked with friends, he quoted verses about heaven and salvation. Before we left for school each morning, he would remind us to let others see Jesus in our lives. Before each service held in our church, he would join two other men in kneeling before God in prayer, giving that service to Him. Dad could be counted on to put God first. His inspiration was implanted in the heart of each of us, which blossomed into love and dedication to the Lord.

When I was very young, my oldest brother, Don, enlisted in the U.S. Army. While he was stationed in Colorado, Mom and Dad visited him several days. With Don gone, Richard was the oldest, so it became his duty to watch over us in Mom and Dad's absence. Even then Richard was handy in practical matters, and had a lot of common sense. He took good care of us, and managed the farm with ease.

Later Don was sent overseas, and there were times when we feared we would never see him again. When he was fighting in Korea, there was no word from him for weeks, and no way that we could contact him. It seemed as though months had passed when we learned that his battalion had been surrounded by the enemy, and there had been no way they could get in or out. Don had been hit several times, but had not been seriously injured except that the noise from the large guns affected his hearing in both ears. He said that often the large guns had such an impact that the candlelight by which he wrote letters would blow out several times before he could finish.

We prayed for him day after day, trusting the Lord to keep him safe and alive. The Lord answered our prayers; Don returned home in 1952. His wife, Clara, drove him home from Battle Creek, Michigan. When he reached home, sooner that we had expected, Carolyn and I excitedly met him at the door. Mother was taking a bath. Don wouldn't allow us to tell her he was home; he wanted to surprise her himself!

My brother Roger and I were very close. As we baled hay in the fields we talked about the things on our hearts and minds. He was thoughtful and would have done almost anything for me. Roger often said, "If you can't get Dad's car tonight, Marolyn, and you want to go somewhere, take mine. I won't be using it."

Roger lived by his strong convictions. He was concerned that he would marry the right girl. During my last year in high school, he and Alma were the first couple to be married in the newly-built Rose Park Baptist Church. Almost a year later, their son, Linn, was born, making their life together a happy home of three.

Even after Roger's marriage, we continued to work together in the fields day after day. Roger loved to sing while he worked and he often sang sacred tunes. Every other day or so, out of a clear blue sky, he would sing, "Oh, that'll be the day, when I die!" I often wondered why he sang the words as he did.

In June 1961, five months after I left for Tennessee Temple College, Roger was killed in a traffic accident. Alma was expecting their second child at the time. Two weeks before his death, he had told Alma that they needed to increase their life insurance policy. As he signed the papers, he had remarked that those might be the last papers he would ever sign. Roger and Alma's wedding had been the first wedding in Rose **Park** Baptist Church; now his funeral was the first funeral held there. The Lord spoke to us through Psalm 116:15 at the time of Roger's death: "Precious in the sight of the Lord is the death of His saints." Roger's death was a great loss, but just knowing our brother's death was precious to the Lord made the burden easier to bear.

Carolyn and I looked just alike during our younger years; even Dad couldn't tell us apart. One difference was that Carolyn was born with a heart defect, and had to take strong medication till she gradually outgrew the problem.

Graduation from the eighth grade was a thrilling but frightening event for Carolyn and me. We were proud that neither of us had failed along the way and that now we were graduating together. It meant much to us to come to this big day, side by side. We had never been separated, not even in the playground at school during recess. It was awesome to realize that next fall we would be attending a big city high school. We would no longer have just five pupils in our class, with only one teacher; we would be among hundreds of kids, with a different teacher for each class. I just knew I would get lost in the halls, and be too scared to know which way to turn. It was frightening, too, that we would have to ride a school bus into the city each day, and then catch the right bus to get home.

That summer passed quickly into fall, and the anticipation of high school turned into reality. The principal felt it best to separate all twins; therefore, for the first time Carolyn and I were assigned different classes. Till now, we had been as one person; we had not lived our lives as separate individuals.

By the time the first weeks of school had passed, we found ourselves adjusted to the new environment, and ready to face the year. Coming from a little country school, we found our city-raised classmates more advanced in their studies. We worked hard, however, and were able to keep up with our class.

Carolyn and I still looked enough alike that we could exchange classes, and neither the teacher nor our classmates would know the difference. Sometimes we even confused our boyfriends. Carolyn had been going with one boy for some time, so we took it for granted that he could tell us apart. One evening when he came to pick up Carolyn, I answered the door, expecting my date. Carolyn's date held a box of valentine candy behind his back, looked at both of us, and exclaimed, "Well, which one is it?"

After a couple of years in high school, I began to realize that we needed to develop individually, separate from one another. We had a long talk about it. I told Carolyn I was going to begin living my life as I felt led, and that I wanted her to do the same. I explained that I would choose my friends, and she should choose hers. We would no longer dress alike, either. She was not quite ready for this break. She understood it was for our best, but I think it hit her harder than it did me.

Both Carolyn and I were Christians, but during our high school years I experienced doubts about my salvation experience. I was deeply concerned about whether I was truly born again. Making sure of this decision was more important than anything else in life. I was afraid Jesus would come, and leave me on earth to face eternity without Him. Conviction plagued me during every church service. I couldn't seem to really believe the Lord would save me.

I talked with our youth pastor, Garland Cofield, about my fear. One day he asked me, "Marolyn, who are you looking to, to keep you saved?" He helped me see that I was not to look to myself, to my weak points or my strong points. God would hold on to me; salvation was complete in Him. I pondered this for many days. I had been so much under conviction that I had not been able to study for months. I didn't want to talk with anyone or be around people. I just wanted to think and search my heart.

Then we went to Yankey Springs for a winter youth retreat with the young people of our church. It was there on a Friday night that I finally received assurance of my salvation. Christ had said, "It is finished," and He could keep me saved. I asked Pastor Cofield to pray with me after services that night, and I asked the Lord to save me if I had never been saved before. God took away my doubts and fears. I knew I was in Christ, and nothing could separate me from that Father-child relationship I had in Him.

When I was sure of my salvation, my life changed. I wanted to be with people and talk with friends. I prayed about everything. My heart was flooded with peace, joy, and happiness because I knew Christ lived within my heart. I was His child, and if He were to come, I was ready to go. I looked back over my life and realized that I had really been saved at the age of nine. I had come to God with childlike faith, and it was then that the first miracle had taken place in my life.

When I knew for sure I was saved, I wanted my life to count for Jesus. Carolyn, however, became more and more involved with the wrong type of friends. She chose her companions from among those who were not Christians or regular church attenders; I chose my friends from among those who loved the Lord. So our ways parted for a couple of years.

In 1959 we graduated from high school and that summer Carolyn searched her life. She decided to go to Tennessee Temple College the following September. Once there, she settled down and began to really serve the Lord. We walked on common ground again, and became happier than ever; nothing could break the strong bond of love between us.

Even though our appearances became less identical, we still often thought alike. Through our letters we found that we had done the same things at the same time: perhaps styling our hair alike, or sewing a dress in the same pattern or color.

We felt sorry for our young sister, Virginia. When Carolyn and I started high school, she began walking the mile and a half to the country school by herself. Carolyn and I had had each other, but Virginia had no one. She often must have felt left out, especially when Carolyn and I would take the car and leave her home, or when we would have so much to talk about, and exclude her. Virginia clung to Mother more and more because she was alone and needed love and understanding. She had a close girl friend at church, but since we lived in the country, she couldn't chum around with her friends like other girls could. As Virginia grew older, however, she was no longer left out of our lives, and we three sisters grew closer in love and respect for one another.

Our family days were happy ones and God honored Mom and Dad's prayers and faithfulness to Him. They saw each one of their children accept the Lord as Saviour, and then go forward to follow and serve God in their daily lives. Donald, Richard, and Victor became active in their churches. Carolyn and her husband, Bill Black, began serving the Lord faithfully with Gideons International, in addition to holding adult Bible classes in their home and a Good News Bible Club at the community center. Virginia became a nurse and an active member of her church.

5

Separation

My childhood had been happy and secure. But what about my daughter, Sharon? How would my leaving her for three months affect her security, her personality, her happiness? As we drove to Little Rock, Arkansas, where I would attend the school sponsored by Arkansas Enterprises for the Blind, I felt an overwhelming sense of loneliness and heaviness for Acie and Sharon.

It was February, 1972. We had contacted the Services for the Blind in Louisiana after returning home from the Houston medical center with the advice to "go home and learn to live with it." Almost a year and one half had passed, and the doctors had been right. My vision had failed, till I had only perception of light. I could see movement and see light through windows and doors. At least I could tell night from day.

Word spread from Farmerville that I was losing what vision I had left. People in Farmerville and preachers all across Louisiana became concerned and asked that their congregations pray for me. These pastors wrote or called us, assuring us of their prayers. It was comforting to know people were praying. Of course, my home church in Michigan was also praying again, that the Lord would give me the strength and courage I needed.

I didn't want to leave my family to go to the school for the blind, but I needed help. For three years I had been unable to see steps. I had to let other people guide me wherever I went. I bumped into people and furniture. No longer could I recognize people by their forms. No matter how well-adjusted I was, I was told, severe personality changes would probably arise as my blindness progressed. Along with the changes in my personality, I could expect feelings of deep insecurity.

It took several months of paperwork before I was able to enroll in the school for the blind, but still I was worried about going. Sharon was only three and a half years old, and Acie was working every day in a clothing store, so he couldn't look after her. My parents would not be able to keep her because they were up in Michigan. I didn't want my eye problems to affect her emotionally. It was an adjustment for all of us, but I was especially concerned about Sharon. Acie and I prayed and prayed, seeking the Lord's will. He answered our prayer! We were able to make arrangements with Acie's parents to keep Sharon. Though both of them were employed, Mr. Ford worked by shifts, so most of the time Sharon would be able to stay with them. Now we knew why the Lord had led us to Farmerville, Louisiana instead of to Kentucky. Mother and Daddy Ford lived only 30 miles from Farmerville and the Lord knew we would need their help during this trying time.

Sharon would be in the best possible place for her, but I still worried for her. Both her parents would be gone; Acie had a full-time job other than the church pastorate and could be with her only on weekends. I was thankful that she could stay with her grandparents, whom she adored, but I prayed that she wouldn't feel insecure, think we weren't coming back, or that we didn't love her. My heart hurt for my little daughter.

Leaving me at the school for the blind was the hardest thing Acie ever had to do, he told me later. He panicked at the thought of leaving me alone in this strange place to which he was an outsider. Yet to me, it was not so strange, for I too was unsighted.

Acie and I had never been separated in our 10 years of marriage, not even for one night. The thought of being separated for three to four months was almost unbearable. We looked for a restaurant where we could talk.

We finally found one and went inside. We could hardly hear ourselves talk above the loud piped-in music. Acie finally asked the manager to turn the volume down so we could hear each other talk. This he graciously did, and with broken hearts we tried to make the most of our few remaining minutes together. All too soon, the time came to say good-bye.

It was difficult, but we knew I had to stay. Sharon was almost four years old, too young to understand fully why her mother could not go back home. Sad and depressed, Acie and Sharon drove home. Acie tried to comfort her by reminding her that she could spend the night with her grandparents.

My first days at the Training Center for the Blind were ones of confusion, loneliness, and anxiety. I was in a strange place where I couldn't see. I knew no one around me. I couldn't do the things I was accustomed to doing.

Immediately after entering the Training Center, I began attending classes. Life was hectic; there was no time for gradual adjustment. We were thrust right into activities. This constant activity was good; I didn't have time to change my mind and go home.

I went to a small-group therapy session that first day when I was feeling so desperate and frightened. Seven people were in the group, and all of us were asked to honestly express our feelings about our blindness. The instructor asked me to tell my name and something about myself since I was new in the group. Then I was asked to tell how I felt about being a trainee. I expressed my feelings of depression, tension, insecurity, and frustration in not knowing where things were located: the doors, the walls, the steps, the buildings themselves. The instructor listened patiently, then asked if I had one particular problem that worried me more than the others. I told her yes, that I was worried about Sharon, was afraid that this long period of separation from her parents might hurt her emotionally. After listening to me pour out my troubles, the instructor tried to help by explaining that Sharon would not become insecure, but that she would be able to understand that her mother was learning to become a better mother. She assured me it was not like being separated from parents because of marital problems.

I wanted to be comforted by her words, but I was so disturbed and upset that I burst out crying. I left the group and rushed to my room, which was just down the hall. Later I came back to the group discussion, but didn't participate. I just sat and listened, longing for circumstances to be different.

Had it not been for one instructor I could not have made it. John Strickland happened to be sitting in the first class, listening and taking notes for a man who was deaf and blind. Mr. Strickland, a mobility instructor, knew exactly what I was feeling inside because he had been blind for four years. Surgery had helped him, however, and his sight had gradually returned to normal.

After that first meeting, Mr. Strickland said he wanted to talk with me. Going right to the point, he helped me understand that my emotional problems stemmed from the fact that I was a normal person in an abnormal situation. This was a great consolation, because I almost feared I was emotionally unbalanced. The multiple losses of blindness had had an extreme effect on how I felt about myself, yet I had to face my blindness realistically.

Mr. Strickland helped me adjust to my new life and understand the reasons for my confusion. As I had become blind, I had gradually lost myself in an unsighted personality: I had lost my identity. Having studied psychology, Mr. Strickland could read people like a book, and because he had been blind, and had known the agony and inner frustration I felt, I could tell him what was on my heart.

Yet adjusting to blindness wasn't easy. When I first became legally blind; with 20/

200 vision, I had to learn new ways of doing things. When I lost beyond 20/400 vision, previous methods no longer worked. Again I had to find new methods of doing things. Then I went totally blind except for good light-perception. I had still another adjustment when I lost this fragment of sight. Insecure feelings arose; again I experienced depression. At first I went through a period similar to bereavement—a vital part of me had died. All the worry or reminiscing in the world wouldn't bring my eyesight back. I had to do what the doctor had said and "learn to live with it." Yet the inner agony tore me apart. My only consolation was in knowing that this was God's will for my life and that He could bring some good out of my suffering. I remembered Proverbs 3:5-6: "Trust in the Lord with all thine heart; and lean not unto thine own understanding. In all thy ways acknowledge Him, and He shall direct thy paths." Even when the going was the hardest, I had this feeling deep inside that I would not always be blind. I knew that God still performed miracles, and that He could restore my sight if it were His will! I also knew it wasn't always His will to answer our prayers by performing the specific

miracle we asked for. I had to pray and have faith in God's direction. I found that by putting my trust in God, and depending on Him, I could "do all things through Christ which strengtheneth me" (Phil. 4:13). I did not ask God *why* this blindness had to happen. I just prayed many times, "Lord, if I have to be blind, please may it be for a reason."

There was a procedure for everything at the center. At each mealtime, for example, we would go upstairs to the dining hall, which had a three-foot-wide strip of carpet all around it. As long as we stayed on the carpet, we knew where we were; it served as a path. Once inside the dining hall, we turned left, and followed the carpet the length of the wall. As I felt the window, I knew when to turn. The drapery established the corner for me. I would turn right and walk to the next corner. We progressed across the dining room by walking along the walls, and actually made a square before we were in line to be served.

The kitchen staff would set our plates on the counter. If they tried to hand them to us, we could either miss them completely, or bump them and cause a spill. When they set our plates on the counter, we knew exactly where to feel for them.

Each blind person was assigned a particular chair at a certain table for the duration of his stay. After I received my plate, I would follow the carpet until I came to the tables. With my plate in my left hand, I would feel the tables with my right hand. I counted tables until I came to the third row. Common sense helped a person find his table.

Unfortunately, everyone didn't use his common sense. Some would be so afraid of spilling their food that they would clutch their plates tightly with two hands and steer themselves with the plate, instead of guiding themselves with their hands. The tables were close together; therefore often when I was eating, someone would crash his plate into the back of my head and spill his food all over me. Often I felt like saying, "If you would just hold that plate with your left hand and guide yourself with your right hand, you wouldn't hit me with your plate."

Four people sat at each table, which was about the size of a card table, and was set exactly the same way every day. The napkins were placed in the middle of the table. The salt and pepper were on the other side of the napkin holder from me. The butter was on the right of the napkins, and the sugar was on the left. My table partners were three men, one of whom annoyed me by getting his fingers in my dessert at nearly every meal. This fellow, who sat to my right, often reached into the middle of the table for sugar, licked his fingers, and said, "Oops, I'm sorry. I got in your dessert again." I wouldn't have minded nearly so much if he had used the correct procedure, which was not to reach, but to move the hand across the table around the dishes to find whatever he desired.

One day after he had gone, I said to the waitress, "Just on this one table, could we switch the butter and the sugar so the sugar bowl will be in front of his plate? This way he will be able to find it easier without reaching over my plate for it." The waitress agreed, but it didn't solve the problem; he usually forgot, and reached anyway.

I found it was a great help to think of my plate in terms of a clock. The top was twelve o'clock; the bottom, six o'clock. (Months later, at banquets and restaurants, Acie, who was a great help all through my blindness, would quietly say, "Marolyn, your creamed potatoes are at two o'clock, and green beans are at four o'clock." He would tell me everything I had on my plate, and where it was located.) This saved me from the embarrassement of fingering my food as I tried to find it, or putting my fork in my plate and having it come up empty.

Some foods gave me a good deal of trouble. Jell-O, for example, was so light I could never tell if it was on the fork or not. Still more embarrassing was to think I had something small on my fork, and then find out the hard way that it was a big piece of meat. Usually when in public, I ordered fish because it separated easily, and was not as awkward as steak, which needed cutting.

Buttering bread was quite a task, especially if the butter was at room temperature. I would reach for the butter with my knife, and because the butter was soft, the knife would go right through it. First thing I knew, my knuckles were in it also. I wanted to give up on butter, but I liked it, so I kept trying.

As I began to learn my way around the Training Center, I found that the things which frightened me most were stairways and steps. When I went up a flight of stairs, I hung on to the railing. I went very slowly, and put two feet on each step before proceeding to the next step. Coming down was even worse. I felt as though I was going to fall on my face. To make a difficult situation even worse, there seemed to be stairs and steps all over that campus. I learned that with blindfolds on, most sighted people are able to go up or down steps without trouble, but the blind cannot do this without practicing and regaining their confidence in motor memory.

After a couple of weeks of my slow progress, Mr. Strickland asked, "Marolyn, when in the world are you going to start walking those steps like you used to do?"

"What do you mean?" I asked.

"You didn't used to put two feet on one step and pause on each one. You put a foot on each step and kept going," he explained.

I realized then how ridiculous I must have looked, and decided that no matter how scared I was, I would master those steps.

Often when I went out for a walk, feelings of panic would arise because of my fear of what might be ahead. I could overcome the fear of chairs or small obstacles that might be in my path, but awnings, low-hanging signs, or tree branches that could strike me across the face were the unknown dangers and difficulties. I needed more motivation than a sighted person would need before I dared to venture out.

Community travel also frightened me. Sometimes as I walked along the roadside with my mind on other things, my cane would suddenly hit a parked car, startling me. I learned that I had to think about obstacles that I might step on along the way, such as broken sidewalks, hills, or thick grass.

I worried about getting lost, wandering too far, or going east when I wanted to go west. I was in constant fear of holes in the ground and pavement, rocks in my path, and toys on the floor. A barking dog became frightening when I could not see his tail wag or know he was behind a fence.

Soon after moving to the Training Center, I added a new accessory to my everyday attire: a long, slender Hoover cane. Its purpose was not to be a crutch but rather an extension of my sense of feel.

I trained for one week before getting my own cane. I was taught how to hold and get the feel of a cane, how to find doors inside the buildings, and how to get to my classrooms by using the cane. Each building had a sidewalk around it which elevated slightly at the door, and then leveled off again. The elevation of the sidewalk established doorways for me.

I learned to listen to the tapping sound of the cane. As the sidewalk elevated or declined, for example, the tone changed. Tapping a small cement square produced a different sound than tapping a large one. Tapping in front of a brick building made a sound different from that produced by tapping in front of a building with a glass front. I practiced over and over until I could distinguish these sounds.

When we went to the dining hall to eat, we always left our canes on a coat rack hook. I could find my own cane after dining because each person was fitted to his or her cane, so someone else's just did not feel right. Each cane also had a chain on the top with a distinctive gadget for identification. Mine was something from my key chain. I could find my cane easily enough, but sometimes someone in a hurry would make a mistake. I would come from a meal, search all the canes, and find mine was missing. I knew if I took someone else's cane, he or she would be stranded, so I would wait at the coat rack, listening for a familiar voice. If I didn't recognize a voice, I had to ask each person who came by if he was going to my dorm, and if I could take his or her arm to get the second cane I kept in my room. Usually the person who had taken the wrong cane would discover the error and return the cane to the coat rack at the next meal.

At first carrying a cane embarrassed me. It didn't bother me at the Center where everyone carried a cane. Downtown Little Rock was another story. I felt that every sighted person was watching me. Nevertheless, as my training progressed, I learned to be proud of my white cane, and to use it with dignity. My eyes didn't show blindness; therefore strangers had no way of knowing I was blind. With my cane there was no question about it. I didn't have to tell them I was blind. I didn't have to wait for people to discover my blindness through some mistake I had made. They could see for themselves. Once I had tried with all my power to hide my blindness. Now I was proud that my white cane testified to that fact.

Once I got over being self-conscious about

my cane, I learned what a great help it was. If I was shopping in a big department store and wanted to find the shoe department, I would tap my cane from left to right down the aisle until I touched carpet. Most shoe departments were carpeted. If I smelled leather, I knew I had found it. To find the cosmetic counter, I walked until I smelled powder. I found the candy counter by following the aroma of peanuts and popcorn. To find the ladies' department, I again felt for carpet with my cane. By feeling the clothes, I could tell if I was in the adult department. I would stand for a minute and listen for the cash register to ring; then make my way toward it. When the clerks were no longer busy, they would see my white cane and ask, "May I help you?" Then I would describe what I wanted to buy, suggesting color, size, style, fabric, and price.

Even though my training made shopping fun, I didn't buy much while I was at the Training Center. When a sales clerk said a dress was green, I had no way of knowing if I liked that shade of green. If she said it had a nice design, I could only imagine if the design were large or small. I missed Acie's judgment too. I had come to trust it so much that I didn't want to purchase any clothes without his opinion. He knew my taste in clothes, and he was honest about what looked good and what didn't.

6

A Sense
of Humor

Once we had settled down at the Training
Center and accepted our blindness, we began
to make friends and use our sense of humor
once more.

One day I was standing by a vending
machine talking to Willard, a friend who had
some vision. Another friend, Donna, who
was totally blind, came down the hallway,
bumped into the machine, and thinking it
was a person, began apologizing in the sweet-
est, most humble manner. "Oh, excuse me,"

she said. "I didn't mean to bump into you."
Willard knew what had happened, and could
not contain his laughter. He explained to
Donna that she was apologizing to the vending machine. All three of us enjoyed a good
laugh.

Another incident proved funny only a
while after it happened. We were in downtown Little Rock in our mobility training
class. We had a particular route to follow,
and a friend, whom I'll call Joe, had the same
route as mine, only in reverse, which meant
that at some point as we walked around our
block, our paths would meet. Joe never allowed himself to learn that a white cane is a
delicate instrument, intended to be tapped
lightly from side to side. Joe was quite
robust, and would ungracefully slap his cane
from right to left. I found myself in front of
a bus stop on this particular day, with people
on the right of me lined up against a building
waiting to catch a bus. Parking meters and
traffic were on the left and straight ahead I
could hear the unmistakable sound of Joe
slapping his cane against the sidewalk!
Whap! Whap! Whap! As Joe came closer and
closer, I walked slower and slower, *Whap!
Whap! Whap!* Joe was whipping his cane

from side to side as though he was trying to
tear the sidewalk apart. There was no mistake
now. He was coming straight toward me! I
tried calling out to him, but my voice was lost
in the sounds of the city buses as they approached the curb. We had been taught not
to make a sudden move when we were uncertain of our surroundings; it was better to
stand still. As I made my "uncertain stand"
Joe crashed into me, cane and all. As soon as
it happened, he called out, "Marolyn, is that
you?" I'm sure it was amusing to the people
waiting for the bus. It was funny to me only
later when I mused how we must have
looked.

Every day at the Training Center we had
a two-hour class in downtown mobility. I
learned that when crossing a street, I should
immediately start across with my cane as
soon as I heard the traffic in one direction
stop, and the cars headed in the other direction accelerate. I was not to pause or hesitate.
Otherwise drivers would begin turning the
corner because they assumed that I didn't
know the light had changed; and once the
cars started turning, I would have to wait
until the light changed again. The whole
procedure was dangerous, but my mobility

instructor went with me until she was sure I could handle it alone.

I also had to learn how to walk in a straight line; blindness had caused a loss of judging balance. Veering too much to the right or left while walking anywhere could be not only confusing but dangerous. Holding the cane in the right position, I found out, had a lot to do with walking in a straight line. I learned to alternately tap the grass at the edge of the sidewalk and then the cement. Later I learned to walk without tapping the grass; there wasn't always a sidewalk to follow.

Blindness also caused me to lose my sense of direction. I could turn around once or twice, and be completely disoriented. I learned to orient myself by the sounds about me. Sounds of busy downtown, street noises indicating which way the cars were going, and the screech of brakes were all clues to help me find my way. At home I listened for the refrigerator or the tick-tock of a clock that always stayed on the same nightstand in the bedroom. Then I would know in which direction I was facing.

If I knew that the dog was kept in a fence at a certain corner, I learned that it could help me orient myself. Certain trees made different sounds as the wind blew through them. Various birds singing in the trees on particular corners helped me find my way, as did the smell of roses in some yards.

The warmth of the sun helped me decide if I was in the shade of a building or a tree. The way the air felt when it came through the break between two buildings helped me know how far I had progressed down the sidewalk.

My nose helped me locate particular stores. A bakery smelled like dough; a pipe store smelled like tobacco. A restaurant smelled like food. A shoe store smelled like leather, a dime store smelled like peanuts; a bank smelled like money.

Often just when I thought I might be lost, these sounds and smells reassured me.

Contrary to popular belief, blindness does not cause a person's other senses to become stronger automatically. Highly sensitive fingers and ears develop only as a result of concentration, not because of loss of eyesight. I worked hard to develop these other senses. Before losing my sight, it was natural to test other senses with my eyes. I would take a dime out of my pocket, and look to be sure it was not a penny. I would hear water boiling, but look to see the bubbles. But now I had to give my other senses a chance to work on their own.

Each sense had to be developed separately, and this total concentration drained me mentally and physically. Eventually I didn't have to constantly give my attention to so many details. As I developed my other senses, I gained confidence in knowing I had not been totally impaired by the loss of my sight, and began to live more normally.

Smelling and hearing became most important. I learned that when I put a cake into the oven, it smelled raw, but when it was ready to be taken out, it smelled fresh and well-cooked. I could detect when bacon was crisp by listening for the sizzles to die away in the frying pan. When pouring water or milk, I could hear the difference in sound as the liquid approached the rim of the glass.

Developing my sense of touch was extremely important. I wanted very much to learn how to pick things up without knocking them over, especially as I remembered an incident that had happened before I came to the Training Center. Acie, Sharon, and I were visiting in the home of one of our church members who had just built a beautiful home.

They had a gorgeous couch in the living room with end tables on either side and a coffee table in front of it. When our hostess served us coffee, she gave Sharon a glass of iced tea and a piece of cake, and left her sitting on the couch with the tea and cake on the end table. I thought, "Oh, dear, she'll have to reach over the arm of the couch to get her tea and cake. Surely she's going to spill her food on that beautiful couch. If I put her food on the coffee table, and let her sit on the floor, there will be less danger of her spilling something on that couch." I walked over to Sharon, and explained what I was going to do. I reached for the tea, but the end table was as slick as glass. When my hand touched the glass, the tea went flying all over the couch! It was Herculon material, so it wiped off; our hostess said it never left a spot. But I was quite upset over it. I thought "Clumsy me! Instead of leaving matters as they were, I had to make them worse!"

That accident taught me the importance of doing things gracefully. When I arrived at the Training Center, I really worked at it on my own. I learned to move my hand lightly and let my little finger be my guide. The touch of the little finger, I was told, was so delicate that it wouldn't cause a spill. After locating an object, I could put my hand around it and not worry about tipping it over.

Everyone at the Center was required to learn to knit and crochet. This was good even for the men; it developed our sense of touch and prepared us for learning braille.

When I first considered going to the Training Center, I thought, "Oh, I'll have to learn braille!" I was so afraid that I couldn't do it. I learned that braille was made up of six little raised dots that, when arranged in different positions, formed every word in the English language, including letters, punctuation marks, numbers, Roman numerals, fractions, and decimals.

Each day I learned one lesson in braille. In the beginning, when I was learning the alphabet, the lessons were easier, and I was able to do two lessons a day. I soon found out, however, that braille is a kind of shorthand. Two dots stood for the word "knowledge." Two dots in any of 12 different positions stood for many different words. Braille required much memorization and I found that one lesson a day was all I could handle.

When I reached my ninth lesson, it seemed I couldn't comprehend any more. I thought, "Oh, dear! I've come to a standstill. That's all I can learn."

My fears overwhelmed me till the teacher explained that this often happened. He said that as long as I was trying to learn so quickly, I could expect this to occur at different times throughout my braille studies. He recommended a break in the lessons. When my mind had absorbed the first nine lessons, he further explained, I would be able to go on. I took his advice, and found that after three or four days rest I was able to continue braille lessons.

Most of the trainees did not take one lesson daily, but I wanted to complete my training in three months. I wanted to get back to my husband and daughter, my church work, and all the things that were waiting for me. I worked desperately every day to comprehend everything I needed to learn.

As I got further into the lessons, I came to another standstill. This time I did not learn any new lessons for one week, in order to review the previous lessons. My braille teacher said I could go ahead two or three lessons, and gradually the previous lessons would fall into place. This just did not work for me, however. I had to learn each lesson thoroughly before going on to the next one.

I learned braille in two months, and spent the third month reviewing it and putting it into practice. I could not have learned so quickly without the Lord's help. Jesus said, "The effectual fervent prayer of a righteous man availeth much" (James 5:16). I prayed every day that the Lord would be with me, to help and strengthen me. I prayed that I would be able to comprehend braille, and that I could develop my other senses and rehabilitate myself efficiently. Philippians 4:13 meant so much to me: "I can do all things through Christ which strengtheneth me."

The Training Center taught us how a blind person could take care of his own business affairs independently by using an abacus. By working with beads attached to a small board, we learned the Chinese way of adding, subtracting, multiplying, and working with fractions and decimals.

In addition to teaching us braille and abacus, our classes at the Training Center also taught us kinetics, the science of dealing with the motion of masses in relation to the forces acting on them. We learned that if we held a book edge toward our face, then turned the book so that the face of it was toward us, we could feel the pressure on our cheek or forehead. We learned to detect a wall or chair as we approached it. Some could feel an object when it was within inches in front of them; others noticed it a few feet away, but this took much practice. Kinetics also told us whether we were walking up hill or down, and whether we were sitting straight or slouched over.

I found I missed much in conversation by not being able to see facial expressions and hand gestures. Before I went blind, for example, just a shrug of the shoulders indicated a person's attitude about what I had said. Often my sighted friends would forget that I could not catch this unspoken part of the conversation, and I would wonder: Did they like the idea? Did they accept what I said? Did they agree or disagree? It was difficult to judge people's reactions without seeing their expressions, but after a while I did learn to detect personality by listening.

I listened for different tones in the voice, for feet beginning to shuffle from uneasiness, for anything that would help me understand the mood of the conversation. If there was a lengthy pause in the conversation, I would wonder if the person I had been talking with had left the room, or was expecting me to say something. I was never sure whether to speak or keep silent. I appreciated those friends who told me when someone new came into the room, or when someone else left. Thick carpet prevented me from hearing approaching or receding footsteps, and I had no way of knowing unless someone told me.

It helped me greatly when sighted people called my name when asking a question or addressing me directly. "Marolyn, how are you today?" made me much more comfortable than "How are you?" which left me wondering if the speaker was addressing me or someone else. I also appreciated the people who announced who they were. I didn't like the guessing games. Once I felt secure in my abilities and had accepted my blindness, I could say something like "Were you speaking to me? or "I didn't catch your name"— without feeling embarrassed.

I had to consciously avoid picking up blindisms: those habits or peculiarities unconsciously practiced by the blind that draw attention to themselves. Some persons displayed blindness by shuffling their feet, standing or sitting crooked, rolling their eyes, or showing no facial expressions or hand gestures. These blindisms interfered with conversations, and set up barriers. I wanted to look as natural as possible, so I practiced using expressions and gestures, and responding to noises. If a door slammed, I looked in that direction; if something dropped, I looked down. I also practiced looking out of the window and scribbling with a pencil. I didn't want to stand out like a sore thumb.

Having been unable to see other people's expressions, I forgot what they looked like. I was now 30 years old, and hadn't seen my own face since I was a teenager. I wasn't sure my expressions were always correct. Usually I would show no reaction at all until I was sure of the mood of conversation. I asked Acie to tell me if I did something strange or peculiar. I knew that by appearing as normal as possible, my sighted friends would feel more comfortable around me.

Sighted people were often afraid they might say the wrong thing, or use words like "look" and "see." When I let people know that I was blind, and that it didn't bother me to talk about it, they soon found out that those words were part of my vocabulary; it seemed to remove awkwardness from the conversation. I never wanted sighted people to feel that they had to apologize for using these words in my presence.

Often when I was crossing a street, someone would come up to me and offer to help. I appreciated the kindness, but I thought that unless a blind person is obviously in trouble or seeking help, it is much better to let him cross the street in his own way. Sometimes a well-meaning person will take a blind person's arm, and push him forward, without realizing that this throws him off balance. Not only does it frustrate him; it often causes him to stumble. A blind person doesn't want sympathy—"I feel sorry for you." He needs empathy— "I understand how you feel."

Every now and then I came across people who questioned my blindness. I would hear them say, "I haven't decided whether she's blind or not—she acts so normal," or "she handles herself so well." It was a compliment to me that my actions did not label me as blind. On the other hand, it hurt to have someone doubt my blindness when I was living with it day in and day out. The handicap was hardship enough without having people disbelieve me.

I came to realize, however, that perhaps people question blindness because they don't know that there are many degrees of blindness. A person can be blind at 19, and still see outlines and shadows and not bump into people and things as they move. The brightness or dullness of the sun and physical and emotional health are other factors. (One day a blind person may feel excellent and be able to read a little by holding the print to his nose. The next day he may feel tired, and not be able to read at all.)

Another reason people may question blindness is that the blind person handles his eyes so normally because he practices manipulating them. My eyes did not show blindness because I worked at looking toward people when they spoke to me. I listened to their voices. If they sounded taller than I, I would look up slightly. If they sounded shorter, I would lower my eyes. My eye muscles worked well because I exercised them every day. I knew that the ability to look toward the person speaking made them feel that I was interested in what they were saying. Before I had become blind, I had talked to blind people who looked in another direction when I was speaking to them. It was so distracting to me. I knew that by looking intelligent, by looking as though I were interested in what a person was saying to me, I was adding to the conversation.

"How did she know that was her husband?" I once heard someone ask, as if I were deaf and totally incapable of any senses. What a misconception! Probably no two human voices sound alike.

When I became blind, I did not lose my ability to think and make decisions. While it's true I had difficulty at first with spoken communication and feelings of insecurity, I continued to do all the things I had been doing before going blind. Often sighted friends and relatives tried to help by doing everything for me. They praised me for doing a most ordinary thing as though I had just performed some great task. But the sighted world needs to realize that blind people aren't abnormal. They aren't helpless beggars, sitting in a rocking chair. They should not be deprived of the opportunity to think for themselves and show common sense. A blind person wants to retain his identity. He doesn't want to be referred to as "that blind person who lives down the street."

People sometimes spoke through a third party rather than speaking to me directly. For example, instead of asking me if I wanted sugar in my coffee, they would ask a friend I was with, "Would Marolyn like sugar in her coffee?" I always answered their questions, letting them know I could speak for myself.

If people didn't use a third party, they would often speak very loudly, thinking that since I couldn't see, I couldn't hear either. Once a group from the blind center went on a tour of some old homesteads. The guide was standing only four feet in front of us, but he shouted at the top of his voice. He seemed to think none of us could hear a word he was saying. Most of us were quite upset, but out of politeness, we heard him out, trying to be kind about it.

I found that attitudes of the sighted and the blind go together. If the blind feel inadequate, have resentment, and do not handle themselves well, sighted people will recognize these attitudes. Those who work at developing their lives find they are not misfits in society. Some things cannot be overcome, but acceptance by others depends on the individual. Blind people need to understand difficulties that sighted people have in meeting and talking with them. Even though a sighted person cannot know a fraction of what a blind person has to cope with, when each tries to understand the other, a good relationship can grow.

Acie was good at handling the fact of my blindness. He always told people that I was blind; therefore I felt more at ease, as did our guests. If I goofed, they would understand, so I could relax. Still, I did my best to look normal, be graceful and have poise.

I realized firsthand that when a blind person has a good attitude about himself, he is not concerned about being seen by the sighted world. He does not depend on others to do everything for him; he accepts help only when he needs it. A well-trained independent blind person can appear to have a strong personality. Indeed, he has, for he has overcome blindness.

I went home three times during my stay at the Training Center. The people at Cross Roads Baptist Church in Farmerville accepted my blindness in a wonderful way. They would joke about my cane in such a way that I knew they accepted it. They didn't feel they had to treat me any differently than they had done before I went totally blind.

At the Training Center I had learned ways of recognizing people. I learned to listen to the way people walked: some people shuffled their feet; some people walked on their heels, others on their toes; some people walked with a limp. I also recognized people by the way they smelled: some used the same powders or after-shave lotions week after week. I listened for the way people breathed. I listened for anything that would help me identify people, such as the way some men jingled their keys in their pocket while they talked.

One of the men at Cross Roads made a game of standing close to me to see how long it would take me to know he was there. It was easy, really, because he usually unconsciously rattled change in his pocket.

On Sunday mornings before the service, I would direct the choir in a brief rehearsal, leaving my cane against the wall. One man moved my cane to see what I would do when I found it was no longer there. I felt a little embarrassed reaching for it and being unable to find it. I laughed and said, "Someone has moved my cane." He gave it to me. Even though I felt a little sensitive about feeling for a cane that wasn't there in the presence of sighted friends, I enjoyed it because they did it in love, and I felt that love. The teasing was important to me. It assured me that I was accepted by the people even after I lost all my sight.

On a few occasions Acie and Sharon came to the training center. How sweet the visits were! Sharon knew I was there because I needed to learn how to do many things that would help me become a better mother and wife. Her understanding and empathy were outstanding. She accepted my blindness, and wasn't any less proud of her mommy. She was such a blessing!

When Acie and Sharon came to visit, Mr. Strickland would spend time with us, talking with us about my blindness and our adjustment to it. He also discussed with us problems that I had in adjusting to my blindness. He showed Acie the importance of "letting me do for myself." It would have been easy for Acie to do things for me; he wanted to be helpful. Yet, Mr. Strickland helped him see that it wouldn't be good for me to become too dependent on him. I had learned to be independent, Mr. Strickland told Acie, and I should stay independent. He made sure we were all aware of the problems at hand, and knew how to cope with them.

Acie never got over the feeling of being out of place at the Center. When we were walking on campus, and I stopped to talk to friends, he felt that I was part of a world of which he could never be a part. Yet, he could see that I identified with these blind people. It was a difficult experience for him.

Also difficult was saying good-bye when the time came. It was especially hard for Sharon, who was never sure how long our separation would be; she could not understand why it was taking so long. She always wanted to sing her sadness away, so Sharon and her daddy would cry and sing all the way home.

It was never easy for Acie and Sharon to come to the Center. Acie had to ask for leave on Saturday, and pay someone to fill the pulpit for him on Sunday. Reserving a motel room was another expense. That, added to travel costs, made frequent visits impossible for us. We were never far away from each other, however, in thought and in prayer. And as soon as Acie and Sharon would leave for home after each visit, I would once again plunge into my studies, trying to learn quickly, in order to finish in three months, so that I could return to my family.

Meanwhile, Acie's burden was becoming heavier and heavier. He was alone, and working two jobs, seven days a week. He worked as a clothing salesman Monday through Saturday, and preached Wednesday and Sunday. In the evenings he had to prepare his sermons and make time for visitation and sick calls. He had to cook his own meals, do whatever house cleaning was necessary, shop for groceries, and take care of his clothes.

On Saturday night after work, he would drive 30 miles to get Sharon. After preaching the Sunday evening service at the church, he would drive her back to Bastrop. I learned later that Sharon made it pretty well through the week, but when it was time for Acie to say good-bye and drive back to Farmerville, she cried and clung to him. It was hard on Sharon and Acie, and on Mom and Dad Ford, too. Finally, with no choice left, they would have to pry her little arms away from

Acie, and hold her sobbing while he left with a heavy heart.

As the days and weeks dragged by, the burden became almost unbearable. Acie was finding it more and more difficult to stand in the pulpit on Sundays, face the people, and preach, when his own life was so depressing and gloomy. He felt as if his heart was breaking. But the Lord was with Acie, and gave him this verse: "And He said unto me, My grace is sufficient for thee: for My strength is made perfect in weakness. Most gladly therefore will I rather glory in my infirmities, that the power of Christ may rest upon me" (2 Cor. 12:9).

I prayed for Acie every day, and called him during the week as well as every Saturday night, hoping to lift his spirits for Sunday's sermons. I assured him that my prayers and love were with him, and that I would be praying for him while he preached. He prayed for me, too, that I would learn everything I needed to learn so I would not have to take an extension. We had always needed each other, and we knew we needed one another now. We were both lonely and troubled over my total blindness.

I had entered the training center in

February 18, 1972, and on May 18, 1972, just three months later, I was ready to go home. I could never have mastered so much training and learning without God's help—I was so thankful to Him!

That day in May was a thrilling one for Acie, Sharon, and me! It was wonderful to be going home from the training center together. Acie was happy that I had learned so much. Mr. Strickland told him he thought it was marvelous that I had learned braille in only two months. He talked with Acie alone one last time about problems that we would have to adjust to.

We said our good-byes to those I had lived with, and then headed home.

7

Home Again

Words could never express the happiness we felt from being together again! Acie was amazed at all the practical things I had learned. He was pleasantly surprised to find that I could take my cane and find my way anywhere—even in downtown Monroe and to the community grocery store.

I began to find my way by locating the church, which was next door to the parsonage. I tapped my cane till I came to the side of the church, followed the church building till I came to the front, and walked toward the church sign. That sign was one of my landmarks. From there, I walked to the corner where two highways intersected each other. I could judge how far I was from the corner by listening to traffic noises. Once there, I listened till I was sure no cars were coming from any of the three directions before I crossed.

To find the community store across the highway, I tapped my cane till I detected a place where the sidewalk had been torn up to lay a water pipe line. The foot-wide strip of newer concrete led to the store, which was another landmark.

If I wanted to go on to visit a friend, I tapped alternately the side of the road (which was blacktop) and the grass. When my cane hit gravel, I knew I had approached the first driveway. I continued till I had gone as far as I needed to go. It was wonderful to be able to visit friends again. Acie began to see how much more meaningful my life had become.

When Acie and I walked together, I took his arm a little above the elbow and walked a half step behind him. Whether he went upstairs or down, to the right or left, he never had to speak a word; I could follow beautifully. My eyes didn't look sightless and unless I carried my cane, people didn't realize I was blind. Often Acie would say, "Just leave your cane in the car this time." Though the cane had become a pair of eyes to me, and was no longer embarrassing for me to use, Acie found it difficult to accept. Soon however, he began to observe how people treated me in stores. Thinking that I could see if I was without the cane, salespersons gave me no assistance. Acie realized more and more that I needed to use the cane to let people know I was blind. He noticed how difficult it was for me to be without it, so eventually he learned to accept it as I had done.

Braille became a tremendous help in my daily living. I used it to mark my music, make notes for myself, jot down appointment dates, prescription numbers, telephone numbers, recipes, and label my canned goods, spices, and seasonings.

Sharon needed someone to read to her. Acie had done so from time to time, but not as often as a mother would. I ordered children's books that had braille on the left-hand pages and print and a picture on the facing pages. That way, either Acie or I could read it to her. These books helped me to gain speed in reading braille, as I read stories, fairy tales, ABC books, and almost any other kind of book to Sharon. Library books were also available in braille, but I preferred to get them on tape, which allowed me to do other work as I listened to them.

Though we were shown how to handwrite at the Training Center, it was never easy to do. We usually made our letters too narrow or we drew them out too far. For this reason, everyone at the Center had to learn to type. In order to communicate with the sighted public, I had to increase my speed and accuracy in typing.

Braille was helpful in keeping a budget book and I wrote checks by using a clear piece of plastic that fit over the check, with cut-outs where the date, the amount, and the signature were to be written.

Shaking hands with people was a real problem for a while. I would extend my hand, wave it into the empty air, and decide that my friend wasn't going to shake hands with me. What actually happened was that as I was withdrawing my hand, my friend was just extending his. We would miss each other completely. While it must have been quite a comic scene to others; it was embarrassing to me. I learned at the Training Center that the matter of shaking hands could be much easier if I would first determine the height of the individual with whom I was going to shake hands. I could determine this by listening to his voice. If he was taller than I, I extended my hand a little higher than waist-level. If he sounded shorter, I would know to lower my hand. Generally, I found this a workable technique. With practice, handshaking became easier and less embarrassing.

When I approached a car, I felt the handle of the car door to determine the direction in which the car was facing. This way I did not find myself trying to get in the car backwards. If someone opened the door for me, I placed my hand on the door frame to determine the direction. Sharon was always thoughtful when we came to a car; she took my hand and placed it on the handle. I could have found it myself, and often did, but it always touched my heart as I knew this was one of the little things she enjoyed doing for me. Indoors, before sitting in a chair I felt the chair with my hand to find out which direction the chair was facing. At home this was not a problem, except in the kitchen where chairs were often moved.

At the Center, I had learned how to sew on buttons and sew hems and side seams. By feeling the material and the stitches, I could do whatever mending was necessary.

Even before going to the Training Center, I had learned to iron my own clothes. I set the iron on the board, let the cord hang over the edge, and guided my hand from the bottom edge of the ironing board to the cord. I followed the cord with my hand up to the handle of the iron to keep from getting burned. I then placed the garment on the ironing board; I could tell by feel whether I had ironed it smooth.

By purchasing appliances from the American Foundation for the Blind, I could do all my own cooking and housecleaning. I had cookbooks, measuring spoons, and temperature gauges marked in braille, as well as gadgets for slicing pickles, carrots, pies, and cakes evenly.

I didn't have to see dirt to know it was there. Everything in the house needed to be cleaned at least once a week, and some of it every day. When I mopped or swept the floor, I found it important to have a set pattern. I took a three-foot square, followed it across horizontally, then came back and cleaned it again vertically to make sure I had covered the floor completely. It was too easy to miss a spot when I cleaned in a circular pattern.

I bought little braille tags and sewed one in each garment to indicate color. This made separating colors for machine-washing much easier. Before I learned to read braille, I had a wonderful little helper in Sharon, who would tell me what color the clothes were as I put them in the washing machine. Whatever we did, we did together. She called it "play work." She even had her own little broom to help when I swept the floors.

Mental discipline was so important. I had to memorize where everything was kept, and make sure it was always in its place. It was easy to lay something down on the piano, go about my housework, and later wonder where I had put it. Even if I put something aside temporarily, I had to put it in its place.

I taught Sharon to play on the bed, chairs, table, or piano bench—anywhere but on the floor. She learned that when she took off her shoes and clothes in the evening, she was to put them on the bed. She knew if she left them on the floor, I would have an awful time trying to find them, and of course, I might stumble over them. Sharon was always conscious of my blindness, and had a good attitude toward it. When Acie would leave his shoes on the floor she would say, "Daddy, you better pick up your shoes 'cause Mommy's going to fall over them."

When I crossed the highway to get the mail, she would go with me. At a very young age she learned to watch for cars. We didn't cross the street, however, till I knew the way was clear. When I had to leave her with her grandmother for a few days, she would always say, "Mama, you be careful when you cross the highway to get the mail." When she returned, her first question would be, "Mama, were you careful crossing the highway?"

I was always concerned about my appearance. I didn't know what I looked like, so I depended on others to tell me if I was awkward. Friends assured me that I handled myself with dignity, used my cane gracefully, and showed a normal appearance. These words gave me the confidence which I needed as a minister's wife, for I went to many church meetings and into many homes for visitation.

Acie was a tremendous help. Being a particular man, he was quick to tell me if anything was wrong—whether my slip showed or a run in my hosiery streaked my leg. He helped me with the right hair style (which I fixed myself each day), and he assured me that my make-up looked natural. I felt confident when I was with him, for I could depend on him to keep an eye on me. He always did it in love because he knew I wanted to know. I wanted to look my best for Acie's sake as well as my own.

Yet this lack of self-sufficiency and personal independence made me feel that part of me had died. I realized that everywhere I went, people would be watching me because I was blind. I prayed that the Lord would help me to have a healthy emotional attitude as I learned to depend on others.

Unlike some blind people who considered themselves victims of circumstances, I knew I wasn't a victim, because the circumstances in which a Christian finds himself never come by chance. I often thought of the many people at the Center for the Blind who didn't know the Lord. It seemed they had no reason for being blind; they could not feel that God had a purpose in it because they were not His children. I realized that the Lord had a purpose in my blindness, and this made it much easier to bear. Ephesians 5:20 often came to mind: "Giving thanks always for all things unto God and the Father in the name of our Lord Jesus Christ."

I began to give my testimony, telling how the Lord helped me day by day, how I could not live without Him. I told of how I had great strength in knowing that "I can do all things through Christ which strengtheneth me" (Phil. 4:13). I could even go through blindness, and continue doing my church activities and most of the things I had done before. I could learn to do almost anything except drive a car.

Everywhere I went, people remarked how I faced life with courage. Pastors began asking me to come to their churches to give my testimony. I went whenever I was asked, and told the audiences how I had come to depend upon the Lord completely.

I praised God for having sent me to the Training Center for the Blind, and for helping me return home so quickly. My life was where I had left it before going to the Cen-

ter, except that with my training I was able
to do so much more. I was able to be independent; I had begun teaching, and directing
the choir again. I was able to take care of my
family and my house.

Spring slipped into summer. Around the
middle of August, while Acie was visiting at
the hospital, he met a man whose 11-year-old
son had been hit by a bus, and was not expected to live. Acie witnessed to this man,
who was not a Christian, saying, "If you want
to be saved, take hold of my hand, and ask
God to forgive your sins and save your soul."
The man accepted Christ and was later bap-
tized. The boy died, but the man continued
in his new-found faith. Acie was thrilled that
this man accepted Christ. He continued on
the mountain top, spiritually speaking, for
several days. We believe this lifting experience had a direct bearing on the events that
followed.

On the evening of August 25, 1972, Acie,
Sharon, and I went to Bastrop, Louisiana, to
visit one of our church members who had
had a heart attack and was recovering at his
mother's home. Since we were in Bastrop,
we also stopped at the home of Acie's parents
for coffee and birthday cake which Acie's

mother had baked—his birthday was the next day. When it was time to leave, Sharon begged to spend the night with her grandparents, so Acie and I returned to Farmerville alone.

As we drove we had a long talk about my blindness, sharing together our deepest feelings. We had accepted my blindness, and Jesus had helped us live with it, but sometimes it became an almost unbearable burden. Being a minister's wife, I needed my vision in order to do my work more efficiently. We had prayed many times during the 12 years of my blindness that God would restore my sight. Acie would pray, "God, I know you have healing power and can do all things. Nothing is impossible to You. You can do it if it is Your will," but his prayer had never been answered.

Each time we prayed I was reminded of the Apostle Paul, who also prayed that the Lord would take away his affliction. But the Lord said, "No, Paul. 'My grace is sufficient for thee,'" (2 Cor. 12:9). Each time I prayed, it was as if the Lord was saying to me, "No, Marolyn, I have a reason for you to be blind."

Around midnight we reached our home in

Farmerville. Both of us were exhausted. Acie picked up a religious periodical, and I climbed into bed. After reading a minute, Acie put the magazine down, got on his knees for our nightly devotion, and began praying.

We both began to cry as he prayed with great feeling and boldness: "Oh, God! You can restore Marolyn's eyesight tonight, Lord. I know You can do it! And, God, if it be Your will, I pray You will do it tonight."

8

The Miracle

Perhaps neither of us was quite prepared for what happened. After 12 blurred and dark years, there was sharpness and light.

"Acie, I can see!" I exclaimed.

"You're kidding," he answered.

I repeated, "I can *see!* I can see the pupils in your eyes!"

Acie thought that perhaps just a little vision had come back.

I said, "Acie, it's 12:30 at night! You need a shave! I can see!"

Acie still couldn't believe the miracle that had really occurred. He grabbed a newspaper, pointed to the large print at the top of the page, and asked, "Can you see this?"

"I can do better than that!" I exclaimed. "I can read the smaller print!"

Acie got excited. "Marolyn, can you see the dresser? Can you see the bed?"

We shouted and praised the Lord for what He had done! Such a miracle was overwhelming. Things had been rough for Acie lately as he tried to keep up with both his church work and his sales job. He had nearly reached his limit that evening when the miracle happened. We knew that God was able, but we couldn't comprehend that something so wonderful and miraculous had happened to *us*.

Jumping off the bed, Acie asked the question again, "Marolyn, you can see?"

"Yes!"

"Praise God! Praise God! Praise God! Glory, glory, *glory* to God! It can't be!" Acie exclaimed.

We were beside ourselves with happiness. "This is heaven!" Acie shouted. "It has to be! Oh, God why did I doubt You?"

Then he turned to me, "Why did I doubt

God? I didn't believe He could do something like this! He did it!"

Psalms 116:12—"What shall I render unto the Lord for all His benefits toward me?"—came to Acie's mind. We were jumping up and down and crying at the same time. I was getting my *first* look at my husband. For the first time, I could see his face, his eyes, his nose, his mouth. *I could see!"*

I ran to look in the mirror. I could hardly believe how my facial features had changed. I had become blind at 19; now I was 31. I kept taking a second look. . . .

We reached for the phone to call our parents. When the phone rang at my parents' home in Michigan, Mother was awake—she had not been able to sleep that night. For years she had been burdened with the thought of my blindness and her own helplessness in not being able to do anything about it. How happy our news made her! She rejoiced with us over the telephone lines. I asked her to share the news with the others in my family who lived in Holland, Michigan and with my twin sister in New York.

Acie dialed his parents, and his mother sleepily answered. Acie shouted, "Mother, Marolyn can see!"

Mom Ford had been awakened in the middle of the night by a son too excited to speak calmly. She asked, "Is everything all right?" But Acie could only repeat over and over: "Marolyn can see! Marolyn can see! She can *see!*"

We tried to explain to Mom and Dad Ford, but we had so little time. There were many other phone calls to make. We wanted to tell the world! We wanted to run down the street at 1 A.M. and shout that I was blind, but now I see!

We called John Strickland at the Training Center for the Blind. His reaction was the same as Mom Ford's; he asked, "Acie, is everything all right?" After hearing the whole story, he said, "That's wonderful! But let me warn you. This might happen a few minutes and be gone. If Marolyn's sight is gone in a few minutes, you have to accept it. Don't get your hopes up. It could be temporary." He went on to explain that many people who are blinded through other diseases temporarily regain sight at times. He thought this might be the case with me.

Yet to his words of warning and advice, Acie could only answer, "She can see! She can see!"

We realized about this time that it was Acie's birthday—his thirty-third. How we praised God and thanked Him for His wonderful birthday gift!

We were so excited we could not get to sleep. Acie had to go to work the next morning, yet, he was afraid to go to sleep, afraid he might wake up in the morning and find it wasn't true. Finally we asked God to help us sleep, and He did. When we woke up at 7 the next morning, Acie's first words were, "Marolyn, is it true? Can you see?"

It *was* true! I could see! Acie called his boss, and said he would be in a little late because his wife's eyesight had come back. When he got to the store, he ran in and told everybody there about the miracle. Acie couldn't sell anything that day. He'd walk up to a customer and say, "You know what? My wife can see! The miracle came true! She can see!"

Acie called me at 2 that afternoon and asked, "Marolyn, can you still see?" He couldn't wait to get home. Home seemed like another world—a world of joy in answered prayer. When his long day ended at 6:30, he rushed in the house, threw his arms around me, and asked, "Marolyn, car you still see?"

Together we praised God! (Acie not only called home on the day following the miracle to ask if I could still see, but he called home every day for weeks after, and asked, "Marolyn, can you still see?" I would answer, "Yes, I can see! Everything is wonderful!")

The day of the miracle was wonderful! News of the event spread quickly, and people called all day long, wanting to know if what they had heard was true. Could I *really* see?

Yes, I could see, I told them as I happily recounted over and over again how the miracle had happened. The doorbell frequently rang as others stopped by to see for themselves if the miracle were true.

When I had a few minutes to myself, I ran to my closet to see what my clothes looked like! I went to Sharon's closet and Acie's closet to see what their clothes looked like. I looked at pictures of my family. In 12 years they had changed. I went to the church to see what it looked like! What a glorious day of discovery I had! What a marvelous, wonderful day!

The morning after the miracle, the sun shone brightly. Words cannot express the beauty I saw. My heart was full of praise to

God for His creation. Later the clouds covered up the sunshine, and poured out beautiful raindrops. How wonderful of God to let me see both the sun and the rain on that first day!

Sharon had been asleep when we called Mom and Dad Ford about the miracle. They didn't tell her that the Lord had answered our prayers, that her mommy could see, till she awoke the following morning. Sharon expressed her joy, then thought for a moment and said, "I can put my little broom up now 'cause I won't have to help Mommy with the floors anymore."

Later that day, after work, Mom and Dad Ford brought Sharon home and came to see for themselves if the miracle were true. When Sharon walked through the door, I saw my child for the first time. When she was born, I had seen only an outline, a little bundle of flesh in my arms. Later I could see nothing. Now I could finally see her—my blond blue-eyed daughter. As Sharon came in, I ran to her, hugged her and said, "Sharon, I can *see!* I can see! I can see what you look like!" I was excited, but Sharon started to cry. I had expressed my joy to her, not realizing that she had her little heart all set on what she wanted to say when she entered the door. Through her tears she said to me, "I wanted to say to you, "Mommy, can you see?" She wanted the joy of asking me if I could really see, rather than having me tell her first. (She has shared our joy since then with many people. She even tells strangers, "My mommy was blind, but now she can see."

When Sunday came, Acie preached about Peter being in jail. (The Lord had led Acie to prepare this sermon even before the miracle took place.) The church had prayed for Peter, and God had sent an angel to rescue him the night before his execution. Peter couldn't believe what had happened to him. He went to the home of Mary, mother of John Mark, which was where the people had gathered to pray. A girl named Rhoda answered the door and became so overjoyed at hearing Peter's voice that she left him standing at the door while she ran to tell the others. They didn't believe her when she told them Peter was standing at the door. (See Acts 12:6-17.)

Acie had certainly identified with Peter. He told the congregation how the Lord hears the cries of the righteous. I led the choir in singing "Amazing Grace" (I once was blind, but now I see). I gave my testimony, and told what great things the Lord had done for me. When I finished, I asked Acie if he would join me in singing, "He Touched Me." People wept unashamedly as they rejoiced with us!

Days later, Acie wanted to call my eye doctor and let him look at my eyes. I said, "Acie, he's busy and booked solid for months. I'll never get in to see him." Acie was persistent and called anyway. The doctor said for me to come in the next morning at 8:30.

The doctor's startling report indicated that my eyes, medically speaking, were the same. The macular was still full of holes; the nerve endings were dead; the mirror in my eyes was like an old-time mirror with the silver scraped off the back.

A miracle had indeed taken place, but as the doctor read the report, I realized I had to face the possibility that I could be blind again tomorrow. My vision could leave me as quickly as it had come back, if it were the Lord's will, but I could rest in the assurance that I would never be blind again unless He had a definite purpose in it.

After receiving my sight, I went through a period of adjustment much as I had done when I went blind. People had accepted me as a blind person and many did not know me any other way. During the 12 years of blindness, I had lost my identity as a sighted person. When my sight returned, I had to find a new identity. I no longer was a blinded person, concentrating on my every move. Suddenly, here was a new Marolyn!

I could now do everything differently. I could see anything without relying on my sense of touch to find out about it. I could accomplish so much in so little time. I could catch people's expressions in conversation. Life had wonderfully changed for me, but I felt lost in the new me. It bothered me till I realized what I had lost; my identity as a blind person. When I realized this was a normal reaction for a person who had once been blind and regained her sight, it no longer bothered me.

Seven weeks after the miracle, we visited the Training Center, and had a wonderful visit with many friends there. We saw a nice-looking young blind man with a brief case walk into a wall. We could only think that except for the grace of God, seven weeks ago, it could have been me walking into that wall.

After the miracle took place, the Lord began to open up opportunities for me to give my testimony, to tell what He had done for me. The news of my restored vision spread all over the state of Louisiana. I began receiving newspaper clippings about the miracle from unknown people in other states. Letters came from people asking for help for themselves or someone they knew who was blind and could not cope with it. I appreciated those letters. It thrilled me to be able to give them words of encouragement and strength: "With God all things are possible! With Christ one can live with blindness!"

Acie and I meanwhile had felt the Lord leading us to another church; we were not sure just where it would be. We had prayed about it for more than a year when the Lord used a good friend, the Rev. Michael Howard, a Baptist pastor in Felsenthal, Arkansas to show us His will. The Lord laid on Michael's heart to give our name to the First Baptist Church of Huttig, Arkansas. Later he visited us and told us about the work of this church. We began praying about it, and the more we prayed, the more we felt the Lord opening this door. By the time the pulpit committee came and Acie preached his trial sermon, we knew it was the Lord's will for us to pastor at Huttig. We moved there in

October, 1972, two months after the miracle had occurred.

Shortly after we moved to Huttig, the people there made it possible for me to return to Michigan to see my family. I had not seen the faces of my parents and brothers and sisters for 12 years. The delight of that unforgettable visit home can't be expressed in mere words. My parents could hardly believe their daughter could see again. I shared my testimony in my home church in Holland, where six weeks before the miracle, I had spoken as a blind person, telling of the training I had received at the Center in Little Rock, and how the Lord had been with me day by day. This time I spoke as a sighted Marolyn to an overflowing church saying, "These blind eyes can now see!" Many friends there had been praying for me for years, and I love them dearly. We praised the Lord as we shared God's miracle!

After moving from Louisiana to Arkansas, I thought I might not be giving my testimony as often, since we were not known in Arkansas. Yet the Lord continued to open opportunities for me, so that I have had a full schedule since our move to Arkansas.

When Jesus healed the blind man by the

pool of Siloam, that man said, "One thing I know, that, whereas I was blind, now I see" (John 9:25). After healing the demoniac of Gadara, Jesus said to him, "Go home to thy friends, and tell them how great things the Lord hath done for thee, and hath had compassion on thee" (Mark 5:19). Certainly the Lord has had compassion on me; He has given Acie and me a whole new wonderful life, and we'll not stop sharing the testimony of that life with others. We will continue to praise the Lord for His loving kindness.

There is no question that God did have purpose in my being blind. So many times during those 12 years I prayed, "Oh, God, if I must be blind, please let it be for a reason." That reason was to give me a message whereby I could give God the credit, and He wants me to give that message everywhere I go. He has given me the opportunity to speak weekly to audiences ranging from 50 to several thousand. I have spoken on radio and television, and in churches, associational meetings, banquets, Christian Business Men's meetings, and Lions Clubs. Through my testimony God has reached down into the hearts of many, and enriched their faith in Him. There has not been a time when people have not broken down in tears. I have spoken to non-Christian groups where people have come in swearing and gone out crying, too broken to speak more than a thank-you as they grasped my hand. I am thankful for these speaking engagements.

My life is God's. I don't know what He has in store for me, but I'll praise Him everywhere I go.

Once when Acie expressed concern about the strain on my eyes—my vision is not perfect 20/20—Sharon said, "Daddy, don't worry about that. Jesus healed Mommy, and will take care of her." And yes, He does take care of me. Though my eyes do feel strained sometimes as I look at people for a long time when we visit in homes or sit in a church service, I could never complain about my vision after knowing what it is like to be blind. I was fitted for glasses to correct my nearsightedness, but no glasses could do for me what the Lord has done!

Publisher's Note

Since the publication of this book, Marolyn Ford and her family have moved from Huttig, Arkansas to Memphis, Tennessee, where her husband, Acie, is pastor of Boulevard Baptist Church. The Fords reside at 2014 Meadowview Lane, Memphis, Tenn. 38116.